The Happy Birthday Book

This Book Belongs To

_____

The
Happy Birthday
Book

Edited by Kevin Osborn

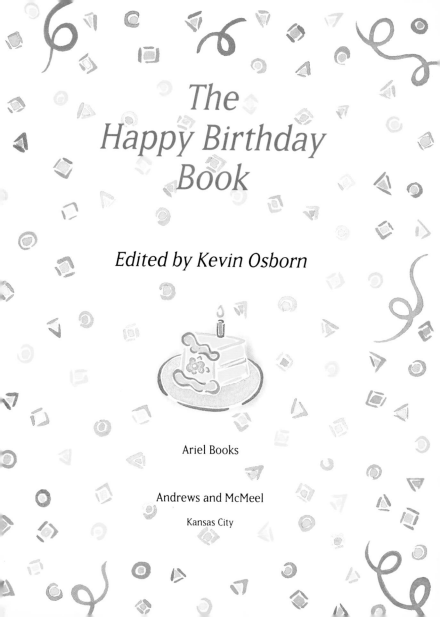

Ariel Books

Andrews and McMeel

Kansas City

Printed in Singapore.

No part of this book may be used or reproduced in any manner whatsoever
without written permission except in the case of reprints in the context of
reviews. For information write Andrews and McMeel, a Universal Press
Syndicate Company, 4900 Main Street, Kansas City, Missouri 64112.

ISBN: 0-8362-4717-5

Library of Congress Catalog Card Number: 94-71137

Contents

Introduction 7

Some Tales 9

Wisdom of the Ages: On Youth 13

Some Customs 16

What's Your Sign? Part I 21

Wisdom of the Ages: Beyond Youth 24

What's Your Sign? Part II 35

You and the Stones 38

Introduction

One cannot have too large a party.

—Jane Austen

There are three hundred and sixty-four days
when you might get unbirthday presents. . . .
And only *one* for birthday presents, you know.
There's glory for you.

—Lewis Carroll

Congratulations! It's your birthday—the one day
in the year that is uniquely yours. Throw yourself
a party—a big blowout or an intimate gathering
with just your dearest friends. It's been one year
(that's 365 days; 8,760 hours; 525,600 minutes;

31,536,000 seconds) since your last birthday and you're that much wiser and wittier . . . and more good looking, too! So don't hold back—enjoy the celebration that is your life. As philosopher and poet George Santayana wisely said, "There is no cure for birth and death save to enjoy the interval."

Some Tales

At the age of forty-one, the poet and novelist Robert
Louis Stevenson learned that a young girl he knew
felt cheated because her birthday fell on Christmas
Day: Unlike everyone else she knew, the girl received
presents only one day a year. Stevenson generously
offered a solution to the girl's dilemma. Explaining
that he had "no further use for a birthday of any
description," Stevenson added to his will a clause that
transferred all claims to November 13 (his birthday)
to his young friend.

"I hope to have the honor of photographing you on your hundredth birthday, too, sir," a young photographer told Winston Churchill after a photo session on the former prime minister's eightieth birthday. "I don't see why not," Churchill commented. "You look reasonably fit to me."

Wishing to send the author and humorist Mark Twain birthday greetings but not knowing exactly where the roving writer was, a group of his New York friends addressed his birthday greetings to: "MARK TWAIN, GOD KNOWS WHERE." Within several weeks, the friends received a brief note from Italy that read, "He did."

After his retirement at age seventy-two, John D. Rockefeller, one of the richest men in the world, learned his family planned to surprise him with an electric car for his birthday. The family wanted to make it easier for Rockefeller to travel about his enormous estate. "I appreciate the gesture," the oil tycoon acknowledged, "but if it's all the same to you, I'd rather have the money."

Elizabeth Bowes-Lyon, Queen Mother of Great Britain, chose to remain active in state affairs well past the customary retirement age. On her seventy-ninth birthday, however, a royal spokesperson conceded, "She has made some concessions to age. . . . When the wind cuts sharply from the east and the temperature of the river is near Arctic, the Queen Mother no longer wades in up to her waist fishing for salmon."

Konrad Adenauer, the first chancellor of the former West Germany, suffered from a terrible cold in his late eighties. A difficult patient, Adenauer railed at his doctor's inability to halt the lingering effects of the cold. "I'm not a magician, you know," the doctor objected. "I can't make you young again." "I'm not asking you to," snapped Adenauer. "I just want you to make sure I continue getting older."

Wisdom of the Ages: On Youth

Being young—who wants to go through that again?

—Dinah Shore

Youth is, after all, just a moment, but it is the moment, the spark that you always carry in your heart.

—Raisa Gorbachev

Remember that as a teenager you are in the last stage of life when you will be happy to hear the phone is for you.

—Fran Lebowitz

Youth is the season of tragedy and despair. Youth is the time when one's whole life is entangled in a web of identity, in a perpetual maze of seeking and finding, of passion and of disillusion, of vague longings and of nameless griefs, of pity that is a blade in the heart, and of "all the little emptiness of love."

—Ellen Glasgow

Youth would be an ideal state if it came a little later in life.

—Herbert Henry Asquith

I don't worry about getting old. I'm old already. Only young people worry about getting old.

—George Burns

No wise man ever wished to be younger.

—Jonathan Swift

This is a youth-oriented society, and the joke is on them because youth is a disease from which we all recover.

—Dorothy Fuldheim

If you want to stay young, associate with youth. If you want to get old quickly, try to keep up with them.

—Anonymous

The secret of eternal youth is arrested development.

—Alice Roosevelt Longworth

My idea of hell is to be young again.

—Marge Piercy

Forty is the old age of youth, fifty is the youth of old age.

—Victor Hugo

Some Customs

THE PARTY

We all look forward to cards, a cake, candles, presents, and a rousing rendition of "Happy Birthday to You," but it hasn't always been this way. Birthday celebrations are a relatively modern invention. The ancients in Egypt, Mesopotamia, and Rome are known to have observed the birthdays of their *rulers,* marking the occasions with parades, circuses, gladiatorial contests, and, of course, sumptuous feasts. The Romans even created birthdays for their gods—staging parades and chariot races to commemorate these great days. Yet the birthdays of mortals were neither honored nor celebrated (and often not even remembered) until recent centuries.

Even today, some cultures do not honor an individual's birthday with parties and presents. Instead, these cultures celebrate birthdays collectively, often through New Year's Day parties. This makes a great deal of sense since birthdays resemble no other holiday more than New Year's Day. Both occasions involve looking back on the past year(s) and looking forward to the coming year(s).

THE CAKE

The birthday cake itself has been part of celebrations for only the last two centuries. The custom began in Germany, where cakes made from sweetened bread dough were coated with sugar crystals. Because cakes play such a prominent part in birthday celebrations, it has long been considered a sign of bad luck in the year to come if the cake falls while baking.

One old custom held that a slice of cake could predict the future. Objects like coins, buttons, and rings were baked inside the birthday cake. The guest who received the slice containing the coin, for example, was guaranteed future riches, while the slice that held the ring foretold an early marriage.

THE CANDLES

In ancient times, people prayed over the flames of an open fire and believed the smoke carried their messages up to the gods. Folklore holds that birthday candles have similar power. If you blow out all the candles on your birthday cake with a single breath, your wish will come true—provided you keep it a secret. An alternative custom involves giving each party guest a candle. The recipient then makes a secret wish—one that will add to the happiness of the celebrant—and blows the candle out.

THE PINCH

What seems a particularly mean-spirited way to celebrate a birthday—that pinch to grow on—is really an attempt to foster good luck. According to folklore, if the recipient of the pinch cries (and you hope not!), he or she will cry all year. The custom originated in the wish to rid the body of evil spirits—and thus ensure many happy days to come.

What's Your Sign? Part I

Do you ever check your horoscope in the newspaper? Even if you don't put any faith in the stars above, this chart will give you the answer to that old question, "What's your sign?"

THE ZODIAC

Aries, the Ram
(Daring and Obstinate)
March 21—April 20

Taurus, the Bull
(Affectionate and Stable)
April 21—May 21

Gemini, the Twins
(Witty and Restless)
May 22—June 21

Cancer, the Crab
(Moody and Domestic)
June 22—July 23

Leo, the Lion
(Outgoing and Generous)
July 24—August 23

Virgo, the Virgin
(Capable and Critical)
August 24—September 23

Libra, the Scales
(Fair and Indecisive)
September 24—October 23

Scorpio, the Scorpion
(Powerful and Persistent)
October 24—November 22

Sagittarius, the Archer
(Honest and Adventurous)
November 23—December 21

Capricorn, the Goat
(Disciplined and Ambitious)
December 22—January 20

Aquarius, the Water Bearer
(Sociable and Idealistic)
January 21—February 19

Pisces, the Fish
(Emotional and Creative)
February 20—March 20

Wisdom of the Ages: Beyond Youth

Do you count your birthdays thankfully?

—Horace

You just wake up one morning, and you got it!

—Moms Mabley (on old age)

He that is not handsome at twenty, nor strong at thirty, nor rich at forty, nor wise at fifty, will never be handsome, strong, rich, or wise.

—George Herbert

Perhaps one can at last in middle age, if not earlier, be completely oneself. And what a liberation that would be!

—Anne Morrow Lindbergh

After thirty, a body has a mind of its own.

—Bette Midler

Middle age is when you've met so many people that every new person you meet reminds you of someone else.

—Ogden Nash

All one's life as a young woman one is on show, a focus of attention, people notice you. . . . And then, not expecting it, you become middle-aged and anonymous. No one notices you. You achieve a wonderful freedom. It is a positive thing. You can move about unnoticed and invisible.

—Doris Lessing

If you persist to the threshold of old age—your fiftieth year, let us say—you will be a powerful person yourself, with an accretion of peculiarities which other people will have to study in order to square you. The toes you will have trodden on by this time will be as sands on the sea-shore; and from far below you will mount the roar of a ruthless multitude of young men in a hurry. You may perhaps grow to be aware what they are in a hurry to do. They are in a hurry to get you out of the way.

—Francis Macdonald Cornford

The really frightening thing about middle age is the knowledge that you'll outgrow it.

—Doris Day

At age fifty, every man has the face he deserves.

—George Orwell

A man shouldn't fool with booze until he's fifty; then he's a damn fool if he doesn't.

—William Faulkner

When men reach their sixties and retire they go to pieces. Women just go right on cooking.

—Gail Sheehy

Being seventy is not a sin.

—Golda Meir

Perhaps one has to be very old before one learns how to be amused rather than shocked.

—Pearl S. Buck

If I'd known I was gonna live this long, I'd have taken better care of myself.

—Eubie Blake (at age 100)

The young have aspirations that never come to pass, the old have reminiscences of what never happened.

—Saki

Age is something that doesn't matter, unless you are a cheese.

—Billie Burke

A woman who will tell her age will tell anything.

—Rita Mae Brown

People who say you're just as old as you feel are all wrong, fortunately.

—Russell Baker

To me, old age is always fifteen years older than I am.

—Bernard Baruch (at age 85)

I can remember when I used to look in a mirror and I looked almost like a schoolgirl. Those were the days when they knew how to make mirrors.

—Jane Ace

Whenever a man's friends begin to compliment him about looking young, he may be sure that they think he is growing old.

—Washington Irving

I'm at an age where my back goes out more than I do.

—Phyllis Diller

When you finally learn how to do it, you're too old for the good parts.

—Ruth Gordon

I used to dread getting older because I thought I would not be able to do all the things I wanted to do, but now that I am older I find that I don't want to do them.

—Lady Nancy Astor

For years I wanted to be older, and now I am.

—Margaret Atwood

It's not how old you are but how you are old.

—Marie Dressler

Old age is the most unexpected of all things that happen to a man.

—Leon Trotsky

All would live long, but none would be old.

—Benjamin Franklin

Old age is the only disease you don't look forward to being cured of.

—Orson Welles

31

We grow neither better nor worse as we get old, but more like ourselves.

—May Lamberton Becker

The longer I live the more I see that I am never wrong about anything, and that all the pains I have so humbly taken to verify my notions have only wasted my time.

—George Bernard Shaw

From the earliest times the old have rubbed it into the young that they are wiser than they, and before the young had discovered what nonsense this was they were old too, and it profited them to carry on the imposture.

—W. Somerset Maugham

Wisdom doesn't automatically come with old age.
Nothing does—except wrinkles. It's true, some
wines improve with age. But only if the grapes
were good in the first place.

—Abigail Van Buren

The closing years of life are like the end of a
masquerade party, when the masks are dropped.

—Arthur Schopenhauer

In youth we learn; in age we understand.

—Marie Ebner-Eschenbach

Youth, which is forgiven everything, forgives itself nothing; age, which forgives itself everything, is forgiven nothing.

—George Bernard Shaw

If you live to the age of a hundred you have it made because very few people die past the age of a hundred.

—George Burns

What's Your Sign? Part II

If the constellations don't interest you, maybe the creatures of the Chinese zodiac will. Were you born in The Year of the Dragon? The Ox? The Dog? Do you share some of the characteristics of the animal that reigned the year you were born? Locate the year of your birth in the chart below to find out. Your sign comes around only once every twelve years in the Chinese zodiac, but for that year the forces are with you.

THE CHINESE ZODIAC

Rat
(Popular, Ambitious, Inventive, and Honest)
1900, 1912, 1924, 1936, 1948, 1960, 1972, 1984

Ox
(Diligent, Patient, Calm, and Dependable)
1901, 1913, 1925, 1937, 1949, 1961, 1973, 1985

Tiger
(Strong, Courageous, Adventurous, and Respected)
1902, 1914, 1926, 1938, 1950, 1962, 1974, 1986

Rabbit
(Caring, Trustworthy, Graceful, and Talkative)
1903, 1915, 1927, 1939, 1951, 1963, 1975, 1987

Dragon
(Powerful, Industrious, Energetic, and Sympathetic)
1904, 1916, 1928, 1940, 1952, 1964, 1976, 1988

Snake
(Wise, Elegant, Poised, and Sensual)
1905, 1917, 1929, 1941, 1953, 1965, 1977, 1989

Horse
(Independent, Cheerful, Diligent, and Generous)
1906, 1918, 1930, 1942, 1954, 1966, 1978, 1990

Sheep
(Inquisitive, Creative, Artistic, and Gentle)
1907, 1919, 1931, 1943, 1955, 1967, 1979, 1991

Monkey
(Enthusiastic, Intelligent, Resourceful, and Entertaining)
1908, 1920, 1932, 1944, 1956, 1968, 1980, 1992

Cock
(Talented, Cautious, Diligent, and Independent)
1909, 1921, 1933, 1945, 1957, 1969, 1981, 1993

Dog
(Loyal, Honest, Discreet, and Generous)
1910, 1922, 1934, 1946, 1958, 1970, 1982, 1994

Pig
(Noble, Kind, Studious, and Altruistic)
1911, 1923, 1935, 1947, 1959, 1971, 1983, 1995

You and the Stones

For many centuries, believers have endowed
stones with magical, protective properties. In
time, twelve of these magical stones came to be
called birthstones. Carrying (or wearing) these
stones (so some believe) can ward off evil spirits
and attract good fortune and good health.
Whether this is true or not, wearing an opal ring
or an amethyst necklace can't hurt.

January: garnet

February: amethyst

March: aquamarine

April: diamond

May: emerald

June: pearl

July: ruby

August: sardonyx

September: sapphire

October: opal

November: topaz

December: turquoise

The text of this book was set in

Matrix Book by

Harry Chester Inc., New York City.

Art by Laurie Newton-King

Book design by Michael Mendelsohn